THE BIRDS

A modern adaptation of Aristophanes' comedy

GWENDOLYN MACEWEN

Toronto
Exile Editions
1993

© 1993 THE ESTATE OF GWENDOLYN MACEWEN

© 1993 EXILE EDITIONS LIMITED

All rights reserved. The use of any part of this publication,
reproduced, transmitted in any form or by any means,
electronic, mechanical, photocopying, recording
or otherwise stored in a retrieval system,
without the prior consent of the publisher is an infringement
of the copyright law.

FIRST PRINTING

Design by MICHAEL P. CALLAGHAN
Typeset by MOONS OF JUPITER
Photographs by JOHN McCOMBE REYNOLDS
Printed by BEST-GAGNÉ PRINTING LTD.
Illustration by MLADEN SRBINOVIĆ

The publisher wishes to acknowledge the assistance
toward publication of the Canada Council,
the Ontario Arts Council,
and the Ministry of Culture, Tourism & Recreation.

THE BIRDS
Gwendolyn MacEwen

CHARACTERS

†

Y: A young black man, citizen of the *Metropolis*

X: A young white man, citizen of the *Metropolis*

SERVANT OF EPOPS: A bird

EPOPS: Half man, half bird

LEADER: An owl

POET

SEER

SURVEYOR

PEKING DUCK

GODDESS

PROMETHEUS

POSEIDON

HERACLES

THE BIRDS
Gwendolyn MacEwen

VARIOUS BIRDS

In order of their appearance

SERVANT OF EPOPS

EPOPS

CUCKOO CLOCK

WEATHERVANE

ALARM CLOCK

PLASTIC BIRD

LE CROISSANT

LA CREPE

HORNED GRUNCHEON

PURPLE-TAILED TERROR

RECITING BIRD

RED-FOOTED MADCAP

SCARLET PIMPERNEL

KISSING QUILL

SHAMELESS HUSSY

STAR-SPANGLED BANNER

TWO-IN-THE-BUSH

LEADER

PEKING DUCK

THE BIRDS
Gwendolyn MacEwen

SCENE

(It is midday on a barren mountain plateau. At stage left there is a single, scrawny tree; at back centre stage there is a large thorny bush; at stage right, some rocks and stones form the edge of the mountain-side, beyond which we have a sheer drop. There might even be a sign with an arrow pointing downwards, which says Sheer Drop. Background is a dazzling blue sky with white clouds. X and Y enter, each holding a bird. They carry a large basket between them, which they deposit close to the rocks).

Y
(To his bird) OK man, — where to now? Shall I proceed to yonder tree in yonder direction, or what? Lead on, bird, or at least speak *up*, fine feathered friend.

X
You crow, you little crow ... what are you crowing about, you little crow?

Y
Look, we're just going around in circles, friend. I mean, we're knocking ourselves out, and we keep coming back to the *same place,* you know? This is what is called, for want of a better word or words, — a waste of time.

THE BIRDS
Gwendolyn MacEwen

X
I don't want to think we've come all this way for nothing. I mean, I just don't want to *think* about it.

Y
(*Sitting down and taking off his shoes*) My feet are killing me. I'm dying, man, I'm dying. To think I put all my faith and hope in a blue-jay. I think I'm losing my mind: maybe I've already lost it ...

X
If we only knew where we *were* ...

Y
East of Somewhere, West of Nowhere — what's the difference? Could you find your way home from here?

X
Home? Don't make me laugh. What was *home* anyway?

Y
Damned if I remember ...

X
Damned is right. Damned are we. Damned we be ...

Y
That bird-seller really ripped us off, you know. Remember when he sold us these two ... creatures? Remember how he swore that they'd guide us to our

THE BIRDS
Gwendolyn MacEwen

destination, our land of dreams, our own private Utopia? Wow, — (that's *two seventy-five* right there) — and where does it get us? *Here.* East of Somewhere and West of Nowhere, —*beautiful.*

(The blue-jay begins to squawk)

Y

I don't hear you, bird, you hear? Ever hear of a blue-jay burger? Ever hear of blue-jay soufflé? Well, have you?

(The bird squawks more loudly)

Y

(Getting up, 'pulled forward' by the bird) OK, where to, bird? Oh no, I'm not going near those rocks! That's a *sheer drop!* Forget it! *(to X)* Do something, friend! What does your crow have to say?

X

Nothing. He's into my fingers again. Ouch.

Y

(Going to stage front to address audience) This is it, then. We've done all we can. Rotten luck. We're lost. This place is Nowhere ... I mean, *West* of Nowhere, East of Somewhere ... I mean ... well, maybe I should explain — *(he crouches down and chews on a piece of grass, looking up now and again at the audience)* My friend and I, you see, are slightly mad. Just slightly. We're trying to find a kind of Utopia, you know, an *ideal* place to live. The

THE BIRDS
Gwendolyn MacEwen

perfect setting, conducive to human happiness, health, and spiritual well-being. We checked out everything, — everything in the *Metropolis*, that is: high-rises, low rises, flats over stores with the traffic outside driving you mad. Lonely rooms that inspire you to do nothing except play games like Monopoly and Solitaire. Everywhere the noise, the insane rush, the pushing and shoving ... the nightmare which we called 'civilization' ... the *Metropolis* ...

X

(Getting up and joining Y at front of stage) Most people would give *anything* for the chance to become citizens of the *Metropolis*. Wouldn't you? But my friend and I, who were born there, are simply dying to get away from it! We don't *hate* the place, but, —

Y

The *Metropolis* is a fine place, a lovely place, but, —

X

(Screaming in spite of himself) Housing shortages. Inflation. Sky-high rents. Insane taxes. Taxes on everything from your inflatable wings to your *crutches*. *(To his bird)* What do you think, friend? Could you sublet your *bird-cage* to me for a month or two? Eh? What about the West Wing? No? The East?

Y

(Muttering to himself) Wage controls, price freezes ... the cryptic language of a civilization which has gone only *partially* mad. The rest will follow. We will not be

THE BIRDS
Gwendolyn MacEwen

there. We will not be there when the *Metropolis* devours itself. It's enough to drive you *nuts*.

X

It's a nice place to visit, but who wants to live there? *(He puts his head between his knees and sobs)*

Y

(Patting X on the back) That's why we've left. We're going to find a nice place, a *super*-nice place, an *impossibly* nice place to live in. *(Addressing the audience)* You see ... my friend and I *are* slightly mad ... *(Pauses)* But we won't settle for anything less than the best. Right? *(He shakes X to restore him to normal)* Right, friend? Right?

X

Absolutely right. *(Addressing audience)* We were told to find *Epops* and consult him on the matter. These birds we have are supposed to lead us to him, to *Epops*. Epops is a sort of a bird who used to be a man, but that's a long story. Anyway, if we can *find* this Epops, he's bound to know something. He's been all over everywhere. I mean, — he's been *around*. He's flown all over the planet, he must have seen *something*.

Y

Down with the Metropolis, down with civilization.

X

Up with anarchy. The bird of freedom is on the wing. The wind is on the bird ... I mean ... *(Faltering)* Where

THE BIRDS
Gwendolyn MacEwen

are we? *(The crow begins to caw loudly)* Hey, come here. The crow's trying to tell me something. *(Y moves towards him, and the blue-jay also squawks. X and Y are drawn towards a large rock situated in front of the thorny bush)*

Y
We must be getting warm, brother. There are *birds* around here somewhere. We gotta make some kind of noise to stir them up.

X
Why don't you kick the rock, friend?

Y
Why don't you bash your head on it, *friend*, — it's thicker.

X
O shut up. Let's get a stone. We can bang on it with a stone...

Y
A *sound* idea. *(He finds a stone, and he and X bang on the rock alternately)*

X
Hello there ... anybody home?

Y
Anybody there?

THE BIRDS
Gwendolyn MacEwen

X

Let's try calling Epops, — you know, *Epops*. He's been around, he's our connection. He's bound to get us *somewhere*.

Y

Hello there. You in the stone. Come in. Come in. Epops, Epops? Calling Epops, — do you read? Epops? Over and out. Well, that's that. *(X and Y stare at one another in despair, until there is a commotion in the bush. The SERVANT of EPOPS charges out of the bush. He is a horrifying sight, with huge feathers and a crown of fiery red maple leaves)*

SERVANT

(Shrieking hysterically) You rang? *Pourquoi?* What do you want? And why? *(X and Y clutch each other in fear)*

Y

Look at that beak, man. He's ferocious, he's *wild*.

X

T-t-t-take us to your *leader*.

Y

Exactly. You took the words out of my mouth. T-t-take us to your leader.

SERVANT

C'est impossible. Il dormi.

THE BIRDS
Gwendolyn MacEwen

X

(Whispering to Y) It's impossible. He's sleeping ...

Y

He's *sleeping*?

SERVANT

Oui. And furthermore, he's *out.* Ha. *Il n'est pas ici.*

Y

(Whispering in X's ear) Ask him, I mean, *ask him.* If his *pen* is on the *table* ...

X

(Whispering) If *whose* pen is on *whose* table?

Y

If his *aunt's* pen is on *her* table?

X

Why?

SERVANT

(Doing a little dance) He is out. He is in. He is sleeping He is swimming. His pen is on the table ... They have not found the *plume* of his *tante,* nor have they found the *table* of his *oncle* ...

X

O shut up. Shut *up.* Look, can't my friend and I just introduce ourselves...?

THE BIRDS
Gwendolyn MacEwen

SERVANT
You're bird-catchers, aren't you? You don't have to tell me, I simply *know*. *(Screaming in a high falsetto)* Well in that case, you're doomed, utterly *doomed*.

Y
No, no, — we're not bird-catchers. We're not even *men*, really I mean, —

SERVANT
What *are* you, then?

Y
(Stuttering) I'm a Fearless, which, as you probably know, is a rare African bird which used to live in a constant state of panic and terror and ate nothing but ju-jubes. Now, of course, times have changed, and —

SERVANT
Never mind all that. *(To X)* Who are *you*?

X
Wouldn't it be appropriate at this point for us to ask who *you* are?

SERVANT
(Obviously pleased at the question and the chance it gives him to elaborate on himself) I? Oh, I see what you mean ... you mean *me*. Oh, I don't know. Let's see, then. Who am I? Who am I? *(Pacing up and down dramatically and putting on ridiculous airs)* Does anyone really *know* who he, she or it, in fact is? I suppose you might say

THE BIRDS
Gwendolyn MacEwen

I'm a slave-bird. Or at least, a glorified servant-bird. Or something. When my master (who as you know, used to be a man) was turned into a half man, half bird, he begged me to become a bird, too, so I could continue to serve him. *C'est la vie*, I said to myself ...

Y
(Whispering to X) He's doing that French thing again. Ask him if the *pen's* on the *table* ...

X
Sssh.

SERVANT
... and I decided that was the only course of action open to me. So I became a bird. And now ... life's a breeze. If he feels like sardines on toast, I head for the sea. If he fancies Vichysoisse, I grab a pot and hightail it to wherever I can find leeks and potatoes. If he's into *soufflés*, I ...

Y
Enough. Do us a favor, and just *call* your master.

SERVANT
Can't. No kidding. He's sound asleep. He stuffed himself with berries and a side-dish of creamed worm. I mean, of course, *vers à la crème*. Sounds better in a foreign tongue, you know. Some things *do*.

X
Oh look, we're getting nowhere. Wake him up anyway. Please, *please*.

THE BIRDS
Gwendolyn MacEwen

SERVANT
(Retreating into the bush) All right, but he'll be furious, — I warn you. *(The SERVANT disappears into the bush. In the interim, X and Y release their birds at stage right, over the Sheer Drop)*

EPOPS
(Calling from within the bush) Let me out. Untangle this bush at once. Do something. This is so *undignified*. Why do I have to emerge from this stupid *bush*. *(Amid much commotion, EPOPS emerges from the bush, covered with leaves and twigs. Skinny and ridiculous, he is half-man, half-bird. He wears a large headdress with three floppy crests, — red, white and blue ... stars, fleurs de lis, maple leaves, etc. He wears a punctured pillow under his clothes, so that whenever he moves, he sends up clouds of floating feathers)*

Y
(Whistling) Will you look at this. Look at those crazy things on his head, friend. Who is this guy, — a walking flag? Or..."is it a bird, is it a plane, is it ..."

EPOPS
(In slightly nasal tones) You wanted to see me? *(X and Y slowly circle around EPOPS, nodding their heads in pity)*

X
Someone's given you a rough time, eh?

Y
Pity, pity, pity.

THE BIRDS
Gwendolyn MacEwen

EPOPS
Are you making fun of me? I was once a *man*, you know.

X
And now ...?

EPOPS
Now, I'm essentially a *bird*, you idiot. Anyone can see that.

Y
What's wrong with your feathers?

EPOPS
Well, some of them are falling off here and there ...

X
What's the matter? Are you sick?

EPOPS
No, I'm *moulting*, you fool. All birds *moult*. Look. *(Jumping up and down sending more feathers flying)* Birds moult. I moult. Therefore, I am a bird.

Y
I'll buy that. That's philosophically sound.

EPOPS
Who are *you*?

X
We're men.

THE BIRDS
Gwendolyn MacEwen

EPOPS

Extraordinary. *Both* of you? How marvellous. Where are you from?

X

The place where they have all those large gray buildings. The place that they call *civilization*. The *Metropolis*.

EPOPS

(After a long pause) Are you officials?

X

God no. If anything, we're anti-officials.

EPOPS

(Sitting on the ground and attempting to brush off his loose feathers) What brings you here?

Y

We came to consult you.

EPOPS

Me? You're not serious? Me, why me? *(Half-laughing and half-weeping)* You're kidding.

Y

(Sitting down beside EPOPS and helping him brush away the feathers) Look, you used to be a man like us, right? And like us, you had piles of debts which you couldn't possibly *pay*. You know ... debts which present themselves in the forms of dollars or of dreams ... debts that eventually detract from the *soul*, or at the

THE BIRDS
Gwendolyn MacEwen

very least, the *character*. *Debits*, I might say. The opposite of *credits* ...

X

(Approaching) Why has he suddenly gone green? Fan him, fan him. *(X and Y fan EPOPS with their hands)*

Y

What I *wanted* to say was ... when you turned into a bird, you got to see all kinds of lands and seas from a *bird's eye view,* — right? You got to see things from the *air*. That means you've got human knowledge *plus* bird knowledge. See what I mean? That's what we need. *You* can point us in the *right direction*. You can suggest the possible Utopias. You're the one who *flies*, man ...

EPOPS

(Pondering) Mmmm ... are you looking for something *larger* than the *Metropolis*? Larger and classier, perhaps? More cosmopolitan? More ... mmm ... *fun*?

Y

Just nicer, man. *Nicer*.

EPOPS

You mean something more ... mmm ... *gentile, refined*?

X

Something nice. Something human, something real, something *ideal*? A city where you can spread your wings and *fly*!

THE BIRDS
Gwendolyn MacEwen

Y
I like that. 'Spread your wings and fly ...!' Oh, I like that.

X
Yeh. A place where your neighbors are your *friends*, no questions asked. Where you don't have to build fences between your property and another guy's. Where you share the wealth and nobody goes without. Where you can have a crazy party every night if you feel like it, — for no reason at all ...

Y
A place where you can spread your wings and *fly*. And chicks, beautiful chicks all over the place with these crazy fathers who actually *want* you to make out with their gorgeous daughters! Crazy fathers who'd be insulted if you *didn't*. Wow.

EPOPS
Well ... Mmmm ... I've been around a *lot*, but, —

X
You must have seen something! I mean you're a bird. Well, almost.

EPOPS
I haven't done all that much flying lately, but, — let me think. *(He chews idly on one of his fallen feathers, like a large quill pen, until he sneezes and casts it away)* A-ha! I have it. Paris.

X
Forget it. I've heard they speak a foreign tongue there.

THE BIRDS
Gwendolyn MacEwen

EPOPS
London?

Y
I've heard they speak a foreign tongue there.

EPOPS
Rome?

X
They speak a foreign tongue there.

EPOPS
Maybe you should just stay where you are. Mmmm ... or if you don't like it *here*, then split. Oh, I don't know ... *(He shrugs, and sends up more feathers)* Why did you come to me, anyway? I'm not a magician. *(X and Y turn away dejectedly)*

Y
It almost makes you wonder, doesn't it? ... that this whole idea of Utopia is *strictly* for the birds.

X
You said it, friend. *(They pace up and down for a couple of moments until they stop dead in their tracks, and stare at each other with 'Eureka' written all over their faces)*

X
What *did* you say?

Y
I said —

THE BIRDS
Gwendolyn MacEwen

X
That's what I *thought* you said.

EPOPS
(Getting up in a cloud of feathers) My God. Mon Dieu. You're *right*. *(Becoming doubtful again and sinking back into a sitting position)* At least I think you are. That is ... Mmmm ... let's see ... *(X and Y pounce on EPOPS)*

X
Come on, tell us, tell us, tell us.

Y
Tell us, tell us, tell us ... *what's it like to live among the birds?* *(Half a dozen or so 'flamingos' who form a chorus line in the Can-Can style, enter stage left and breeze out at stage right, over the 'Sheer Drop' sign)*

CHORUS LINE
(Singing) Tell us, tell us, tell us, tell us,
Tell us, tell us, tell us, tell us, —
What's it like to live among the birds ...?

EPOPS
What was that? Who were they? Oh well, let's see. Mmmm ... what's it like to live among the birds? Hmmm. *(He shrugs)* Well, for one thing ... you don't have to carry a wallet!

X
That rules out pick-pockets. But, —

THE BIRDS
Gwendolyn MacEwen

EPOPS
Think man, think. If you don't have to carry a wallet, then you don't have to carry all those cards that tell the world who you are, or who you're *supposed* to be.

CHORUS LINE
(Re-entering stage right and exiting stage left) Tell us, Tell us, tell us, tell us,
Tell us, tell us, tell us, tell us, —
What's it like to live among the birds ...?

EPOPS
Who *are* those creatures? *(Shrugging)* Well, anyway, — let's see. What's it like to live among the birds? Mmmm ... your *food* is pretty well taken care of. The gardens are full of eggplants and *exquisite* berries ... not to mention poppies, mint, parsley, sage, rosemary and thyme ... *(He pauses and remembers the song Marlboro Fair, which he sings)* Parsley, sage, rosemary and thyme. Remember me to one who lives there. She once was a true love of mine ... *(Remembering himself)* That was, of course, à propos of nothing. Hmmm ... what was I saying anyway?

X
You were telling us about the availability of food if one is living among the birds.

EPOPS
Exactly. I was just testing your powers of recall. Well, there's just about anything you could ever want in the fields and gardens of the world ... *(Picking a few twigs from the nearby bush and chewing on them)* For

THE BIRDS
Gwendolyn MacEwen

full-course meals, for feasting, or snacking, or whatever. Not to mention stuff for powerful *herbal remedies* ... your valerian, your skullcap, your burdock, your moose-jaw, your worm-wort, your slippery elm bark, your dragon's blood, your squaw root, your flin-flon, your ... *(His voice fades away; he seems dazed, or high. He examines the twigs he's been chewing on)* I wonder what that stuff was? ... I haven't tried that bush before. It's pretty ... powerful ... *(He keels over and lies flat on his back)*

Y
(Rushing over to X and grabbing his shoulders in excitement) A fabulous idea is sprouting in my head, friend. Listen to this. Are you ready? We could actually make the birds the *masters of the world*.

(There is a long pause. X Stares at Y, horrified)

X
You're off your rock. You've flown your coop. Birdbrain.

Y
No, you're wrong. Listen to me. I've got a vision. I see, I see— *a city*.

EPOPS
(Slowly coming out of his stupor) A city? Where, where?

Y
(Assuming the commanding stance of a Columbus, and pointing towards the Sheer Drop sign) Yonder.

THE BIRDS
Gwendolyn MacEwen

              X
That sign says Sheer Drop. That's what it says. It doesn't say 'City'.

          EPOPS
(To X, in a loud whisper) I think he's building castles in the air. What do you think?

              Y
Come on. I'll show you what I mean.

(X and EPOPS follow him to the Sheer Drop sign)

              Y
It's obvious. It's staring us in the face. *(To EPOPS)* Look down, down over the rocks ...

          EPOPS
Allright, I'm looking down.

              Y
Now look up. Straight up.

          EPOPS
Allright, I'm looking straight up.

              Y
Now turn your head around in circles.

          EPOPS
I *am*. Oh, my neck, my neck.

THE BIRDS
Gwendolyn MacEwen

Y
Now, tell me, — *what have you seen?*

EPOPS
Nothing. Everything. Clouds and sky. Sky and clouds. Cloudy skies. The forecast is semi-overcast skies with intermittent showers ending sometime this afternoon. Or, showers interrupted by intermittent patches of blue ... however you take your weather ... *(Drowsily)* ... one thing you can always count on, — there'll always be weather ...

Y
(Despondently) You didn't see my vision. You didn't see the City.

X
(Gazing out over the Sheer Drop sign) Do you mean ... all that out there? All that sky, and all that air, all that *space*? That's bird country, friend ... the domain of our fine feathered friends. Layers of air between earth and heaven. I don't see your vision. I don't see any City ...

Y
(Muttering to himself) We could lay siege to their needs, their highest ideals. We could starve them out...

X
Who?

THE BIRDS
Gwendolyn MacEwen

Y
The rest of the world, that's who. And even the gods, the false, uncompromising gods ...

(Something in his tone makes the other two take notice)

EPOPS
(Slowly) Tell me about your vision ... I'm all ears ...

X
Come on ... what have you seen?

(EPOPS and X position themselves and await Y's answer)

Y
Look, — the *air* is between heaven and earth, right? I mean, the air is a sort of buffer zone between what we call 'the gods' and what we call 'man'. OK. *(Pausing)* Now, when we want to go somewhere, — that is, *horizontally*, — we have to get a thing called a *visa*, right? *(Looking intensely at the other two and pausing for effect)* Well, what if somebody wants to go straight up, or straight down? Who controls that buffer zone between heaven and earth? Who is in a position to issue visas to the envoys from the gods to men?

EPOPS
(Considering for a moment) Why, — the birds, of course.

X
Right on. The birds.

THE BIRDS
Gwendolyn MacEwen

Y

The *birds*.

EPOPS

I love it. *Les oisxeaux. Les oisxeaux. (Stopping, as seized by a dreadful thought)* Wait a minute. I'm not sure that I like this. How does it *work*?

Y

Look at you ... you're all in a flutter. *Listen,* — it works like this: when men sacrifice to the gods,— (whichever gods) — the smoke from their sacrifices travels *upwards*. If you control the air, let's say, — then you demand a sort of tribute for allowing the smoke to pass through your territory. Got that? No, you haven't got it. OK, listen. If the aforesaid tribute, or tax, or whatever is *not* paid,— then you exercise your absolute rights and *refuse to permit the smoke to pass through*. Without the smoke from the sacrifices, the gods will starve. Now do you get it?

X

I'm starting to. And then what happens...?

Y

Easy. The gods give in.

X

Just like that?

Y

Just like that. And the birds become the masters of the world, the heavens, everything ...

THE BIRDS
Gwendolyn MacEwen

X
I'm *trying* to understand your vision. I want to see the City ...

EPOPS
So do I ...

Y
Look then. Look at the mighty highways of the sky.

(There is a long silence, as all three gaze upward)

EPOPS
(Dancing around in delight, creating more clouds of feathers) I'm so excited, I could *fly*. Well, almost, anyway ... I think you have a brilliant idea, and the fact that I don't really understand it doesn't make it any less brilliant. *Ah, mon ami, mon ami.* We could make beautiful music, you and I. *(Pausing and becoming thoughtful)* But wait ... is there something here I do not really see? Something strange and dangerous? Something that upsets ... Mmmm ... the thing we call reality?

X
Never mind. We must assemble *all* the birds, and outline to them... the *plan* ... *(gazing at Y)* What *is* the plan? And who should outline it to them?

Y
The plan is to separate.

THE BIRDS
Gwendolyn MacEwen

EPOPS

(After a long pause) To separate *what* from *what*?

Y

To separate the domain of the birds from the rest of the world, so that the birds don't have to answer to anyone, — men or gods.

X

I love it. I don't completely understand it, but I love it. I believe we've found Utopia. So you and I, friend, will outline the Plan to the rest of the birds. Wait, — how do we *assemble* the rest of the birds?

EPOPS

I'll do that. We have a sort of a standard language which they all understand. They still retain, of course, their separate dialects ... *(Crashing back into the Bush amidst a chaos of twigs and feathers)* Stand by. I'll assemble everybody, all the leaders of the various groups ... *(Much noise-making, singing, crowing or whatever emerges from the Bush)*

Y

See any birds yet?

X

No, but my eyes are peeled.

Do you think he's really calling the birds? Or is he putting us on?

THE BIRDS
Gwendolyn MacEwen

(A tall, absurd bird with a clock on its head sneaks up behind X)

X

Frankly, I'm beginning to think that he was merely *demented*. Off his rocker, you know. Cuckoo. What are you flapping your arms around like that for?

(Y is frantically trying to indicate to X that he must turn around)

X

What? Is there something behind me? *(He turns around: freezes, then looks back to Y)* Did you see that? I didn't see that. I didn't see that. Did you see *that*?

(The bird, curious, slowly walks around X, then proceeds to investigate Y)

Y

(Trying to control his panic) Back off, bird. I mean, just back off.

(EPOPS emerges from the Bush with the usual chaos of twigs and feathers)

EPOPS

Ah, I see you've met my friend *The Cuckoo Clock*. He's a handsome devil, isn't he? And really quite rare.

X

Rare. Why doesn't he make himself scarce. Ha ha. Time is of the essence. Ha.

THE BIRDS
Gwendolyn MacEwen

(The stage is suddenly lit up with lightning. Thunder follows. A thin, golden bird enters, swinging its body from side to side)

EPOPS
And here comes another old friend of mine ... *The Weathervane.* How *are* you, you silly thing. One thing you can always count on, — there'll always be weather.

X *and* Y
You said that before.

(An incredible assortment of weird and wonderful birds enter, one by one, like models in a fashion show. The first one carries a bell. The last one, the LEADER, is an owl)

EPOPS
Oh it's you, you nasty thing. *Alarm Cock.* And here come Plastic Bird, Metal Bird, Le Croissant, La Crepe, Horned Gruncheon, Purple-Tailed Terror, Reciting Bird, Red-Footed Madcap, Scarlet Pimpernel, Kissing Quill ... Oh, and two more, — Shameless Hussy and Star-Spangled Banner. Oh, and I mustn't forget our friend Two-in-the-Bush.

(Four eyes twinkle from the Bush; Two-in-the-Bush giggles hysterically. X and Y back away towards the edge of the cliff)

X
Do you think any of them are hostile?

THE BIRDS
Gwendolyn MacEwen

KISSING QUILL
(Strolling up to X and leaning against him) Hi, sexy ...

EPOPS
And now may I present the Leader of the birds.

LEADER
(Silencing the birds with a single gesture) Have I to understand that we have been summoned her by you, Monsieur, on a matter of some import?

EPOPS
I have news which concerns all of us. These two clever beings came here to consult me ...

LEADER
(Regarding X and Y with distaste) Who, them?

EPOPS
Yes, them. They came here from the world of men to propose to us an absolutely fantastic scheme ... *(The birds become highly agitated, all trying to speak at once)*

BIRDS
Traitor! What do we want from the world of men. And what do you know, anyway, — half-*bird*, half-man. *(They lunge forward to attack EPOPS)*

LEADER
Stop. (They all stop) As for the traitor, we will deal with him later. *(Pausing)* But the two beings from the

THE BIRDS
Gwendolyn MacEwen

world of men will be punished *immediately*. How did they come here in the first place? Why did they come here in the first place? *(X and Y cower at the edge of the Sheer Drop)*

X
This is it, friend. We've had it.

LEADER
(Screaming) T-t-t-t-tear them to pieces. T-t-tar and feather them. *(The birds form a tightly-knit circle and prepare to attack. The LEADER stands in front of them, wings flapping)*

BIRDS
Forward. Attack. Fling yourselves on the enemy. Surround him on all sides. Use beaks, beaks. Peck at random. Peck at will.

LEADER
(Enraged) Will you, for once, let *me* do the talking. *(The birds quieten down)* That's better. Now, — Forward. Attack. Fling yourselves on the enemy. Surround him on all sides. Use beaks. Peck at will. You, — take your left flank and engage their right. You,—take your right and engage their left. *Forward.*

CUCKOO CLOCK
(Advancing) No prisoners.

(The birds advance en masse)

THE BIRDS
Gwendolyn MacEwen

X
(Quickly extracting from the basket, the following: a beaver pelt, a large maple leaf, and a large fleur-de-lis) Quick. To arms.

Y
What arms, man? Are you crazy?

X
Here, — grab one of these ... any one.

Y
(Grabbing a maple leaf) Allright, but I don't understand ...

X
These are *symbolic*, friend. And these birds are very superstitious. Trust me. *(X and Y brandish their 'arms' in the face of the attacking birds)*

Y
Oh, this is brilliant, just brilliant.

LEADER
Charge. *(Stopping dead in his tracks)* No, wait, wait.

CUCKOO CLOCK
Attack on all fronts at once.

THE SCARLET PIMPERNEL
(Holding him back) Our leader says wait. We wait.

THE BIRDS
Gwendolyn MacEwen

LEADER
(Obviously befuddled) Look, I said Attack, and I meant Attack, but ... first of all, er, — couldn't we dispose of the enemy's *feeble weapons*? I refer to, — of course — the wholly ambiguous *leaf* which our black friend clutches to his breast.

Y
(Dropping his maple leaf) It seems to me that it served no purpose, anyway ...

LEADER
The skin of the animal you carry, — drop it also.

X
(Dropping the beaver pelt) It seems to me that it served no purpose anyway ...

LEADER
And now, — attack on all fronts.

X
(Waving the fleur-de-lis) Oh no you don't.

LEADER
(Motioning for the BIRDS to halt) I said Attack and I meant Attack. But first, — we must get *the flower which is held in the hand of the enemy.*

X
Not until we agree that *la plume est surla table, mon ami.*

THE BIRDS
Gwendolyn MacEwen

LEADER
Is this a threat? I will not agree that *the pen is on the table*. I will never agree.

Y
(To X) Ask him about *the pen of his aunt*.

X
Oh, shut up.

EPOPS
(To LEADER) Oh look, you're being unreasonable. Why do you want to kill these men?

LEADER
Because they're there.

EPOPS
These men have some fabulous ideas. *A wise bird learns from his enemies ... learns many things ...*

LEADER
Like what?

X
Like how to defend himself. How to become more powerful ...

Y
Yeh. Who taught cities to build walls?

X
The enemy.

THE BIRDS
Gwendolyn MacEwen

Y
But in this case, man, — we are not the enemy. *(Pointing to EPOPS) He* knows, — he'll tell you ...

THE SCARLET PIMPERNEL
Who *cares*? Tear them to shreds.

THE CUCKOO CLOCK
Forward. Time is of the essence.

EPOPS
(Bopping the CUCKOO CLOCK on the head) Oh shut up.

LEADER
OK, well ... I'm a bird of the world, you know. And I'm curious. I do not normally welcome outside views on internal affairs, but I confess I'm suddenly *interested* in what you two have to say. Allright. *(Nodding to X and Y)* Let's hear it. First of all, where are you from?

X
Out West.

LEADER
Etrangers. Eh bien, — what brings you here?

Y
We were being suffocated by *civilization*, friend. I mean, *crucified*.

X
We love freedom. We want to be like you, like birds. We want to fly, fly through the fabulous skyways of

THE BIRDS
Gwendolyn MacEwen

our minds, to bend with the wilful, voluptuous wind ...

LEADER
(*To EPOPS*) What's he talking about? (*EPOPS shrugs. LEADER turns back to X and Y*)

LEADER
That's very nice, but what do you intend to *do* here? What are your plans?

EPOPS
(*Breaking in with a nervous exuberance*) They've already told me. They've got this wild, wonderful, incredible plan. (*Pausing*) I'm not sure if I like it, really. (*Scratching his head*) But I have a feeling that *you* will ... Hmmm ... what do I *mean*?

X
(*Impatiently*) Listen, — you can't imagine what we've thought of. *Everything* will be for the birds, — everything. Look to the left, to the right, look up, look down, — it's all going to be *ours*.

LEADER
Ours?

Y
He means *yours*. (*Poking X with his elbow*)

LEADER
(*To EPOPS*) They're cuckoo. Or are they?

THE BIRDS
Gwendolyn MacEwen

EPOPS

(Chuckling) Most likely they're completely sane, — if there is such a thing as 'complete sanity'. Yes, I think they are completely sane, but *(Pausing) dangerous ...*

LEADER

Dangerous? That's like the word *'exciting'*. Dangerous? *Dangereux*. Tell me more ... *(Nodding to X and Y) ...* my fine, freckled friends.

Y

(Composing himself, as though rehearsing what he's about to say) I grieve for you, you splendid creatures. I grieve for your former glory. You magnificent denizens of the earth, who once were *kings*.

ALARM COCK

What's a *denizen*? Is that some new kind of bird?

EPOPS

Over whom were we kings?

LEADER

We were kings? Over whom?

Y

Over just about *everything*, man. I mean, rulers of the *world*, meaning mankind and whatever else inhabited the planet. It has been suggested ... that you once ruled *Zeus himself*. (PLASTIC BIRD AND METAL BIRD faint, THE HORNED GRUNCHEON, and THE RED-FOOTED MADCAP *run around in circles crying* 'Blasphemy, Blasphemy')

THE BIRDS
Gwendolyn MacEwen

X
(Warming to the subject) Yes. Your race is older than Saturn, older than the Titans, older, possibly, than the *Earth*.

LEADER
Funny, I didn't know that ...

X
That's because you haven't read your *Aesop*. According to him, the lark was born before all other creatures.

EPOPS
(Muttering to himself) Hmmm, a moot point. It's really a question of which came first ... the chicken or the egg. How *was* the lark born, then?

KISSING QUILL
(Sidling up to EPOPS and nudging him) The *stork* sent him, silly ...

LEADER
I find your theory puzzling, but seductive ...

Y
Think about it. If the birds existed before the earth, and possibly before the *gods* ... who then can claim the right to be kings of the world?

KISSING QUILL
(Flirting with X) Hi there, *sexy* ...

THE BIRDS
Gwendolyn MacEwen

THE SCARLET PIMPERNEL
(Attempting to deliver a Karate chop to Y's head) The birds, the birds. Goodbye, goodbye. Let's have no further *adieu*. Truth, truth, — in one fell swoop. *(X fights off KISSING QUILL and Y disposes of SCARLET PIMPERNEL with a resounding slap)*

Y
I re-phrase my question. Who then, has the right to demand a privileged independence from the rest of the denizens of earth?

ALARM COCK
What the Hell's a *denizen*? *(His alarm goes off, and a couple of birds come to the rescue, clapping their wings over his head to stop the noise)*

LEADER
(Considering) 'A privileged independence'. I like the sound of that. But, you know, — Zeus is not going to give in to such a revolutionary plan so easily. I mean, the Almighty is not going to hand over His sovereignty to a woodpecker. *(Glancing at ALARM COCK)* Or even to such as you, Alarm Cock, Controller of the Morning, Minister of Daylight ...

ALARM COCK
(Angrily) I get the farmers up, don't I? I exert my formidable powers to this very day. Consider the factory workers and the office workers and the tradesmen, and yes, — even the politicians, who are still completely in my power.

THE BIRDS
Gwendolyn MacEwen

EPOPS
I personally don't like cocks that go off too early, especially when I'm trying to sleep in, which is almost always ...

Y
Think of what I said. *A privileged independence* ...

LEADER
(Walking around in slow, thoughtful circles) Mon Dieu, mon dieu, *can it be?* (PLASTIC BIRD *and* METAL BIRD *get up and follow so closely behind him that they are almost tripping over one another*)

Y
(Very persuasively) Anything can be if you want it to be, if you want it badly enough. And ... who are the gods? Eh? Who are the gods? Even they have to wear huge headdresses in the shape of birds, to make themselves look mightier and more mysterious than they really are. Zeus himself is shown standing with an eagle on his head, — can you imagine. And Athena wears an owl on hers ...

LEADER
(Stopping in his tracks, so that PLASTIC BIRD *and* METAL BIRD *bump into his back and promptly fall to the ground)* You're not serious? Athena wears an effigy of *me* on her head? Outrageous. Outrageous.

EPOPS
It makes one wonder what the gods are doing in *heaven*, of all places. *(Looking around at the birds)*

THE BIRDS
Gwendolyn MacEwen

Doesn't it, *Crêpe*? Doesn't it, *Croissant*? *(LA CREPE and LE CROISSANT chatter in squeaky voices to one another)*

EPOPS
What do you think of all this, *Two-In-The-Bush*? *(TWO-IN-THE-BUSH blinks his four eyes furiously)*

Y
(Pressing his advantage with LEADER) And what about men. Yes, oh yes, *men* ... my own fellow beings, my ... *(Sighing deeply)* ... my brothers ... my hopeless, human brothers ... *(X puts his arm around Y and they share a moment of silent grief over the folly of the rest of mankind)* *(Y screaming)* They have reduced you to nothing. They throw stones at you, they shoot you with their ungodly little bullets. They're so jealous of your ability to fly, that they'll do *anything* to bring you down. Yeh, — and then they sell you, and buyers poke your guts to see if you're fat enough. And then *they* take you home and roast you, after they've stuffed your gut with breadcrumbs and sage. And when you're roasting, they pour their yukky greasy stuff, boiling hot, all down your back. Yeh. They call it *GRAVY*. *(Pausing for effect)* And that's for starters. Other things happen when you're *fried*, or *boiled* ...

THE RED-FOOTED MADCAP
(Bursting into tears) Stop it. I can't take anymore. You beast, you fiend. You fiendish beast. *(Hysterically attacking Y with her claws. Two other birds carry her out, still screaming)*

THE BIRDS
Gwendolyn MacEwen

LEADER
(Turning to Y and X) I would like to hear what you have in mind as regards, shall we say, a possible *Utopia*.

X
(Turning to Y to receive Y's go-ahead) Allright. Here's what we suggest. All the birds should congregate at some pre-arranged place, and ... *(Are you listening?)* ... construct an enormous wall. A wall that will *enclose and capture the region of space between earth and heaven.*

EPOPS
(After a long silence) Stunning. What does it mean?

THE PURPLE-TAILED TERROR
(Stepping forward) It *means*, you twit, that the foresaid wall will *enclose and capture the region of space between earth and heaven ....*

EPOPS
And what is the region of space between earth and heaven, my friend, — you purple-tailed terror?

THE PURPLE-TAILED TERROR
You fool. You fledgling. You silly thing. Don't tear your feathers. You know the answer.

EPOPS
Of course I do. But just to make sure everyone here is tuned in to what's going on ... I'd like to ask, — OK, *you*, Reciting Bird. Since you know everything ...

THE BIRDS
Gwendolyn MacEwen

what is the region of space between earth and heaven?

RECITING BIRD
(Stepping forward formally) The region of space between earth and heaven is, of course, the realm of the birds.

Y
When the *wall* is finished, you claim your *empire* for yourselves: Do you get it? If Zeus refuses to grant you your territorial rights, you declare a holy war. Yes, — a holy war. You *boycott the gods*. You don't permit them to pass through your territories on their way to earth. The gods will have to have *passports*, get it?

LEADER
(Dancing around in circles) What a terrifying, astounding idea. I love it, I love it. It makes me want to go to bed, and weep for joy, then sleep, and then, perchance to dream *astounding dreams* ...

Y
(Following him around in his circles) Then, — you send a messenger down to the humans on earth, to proclaim that the *birds* are the new rulers of the universe. So, if men want to make sacrifices, — they must first sacrifice to *you*, — and *after* to the gods.

LEADER
And how is that supposed to be arranged?

THE BIRDS
Gwendolyn MacEwen

X
(Joining Y in walking around in circles) Simple! You tell the humans that they must appoint a bird to every 'god'. Some gods already have birds connected with them ... Poseidon has a duck, for instance. Heracles, who's almost a god, has a gull. They're both crazy about honey-cakes, —Heracles and the gull, I mean. So you see? Heracles doesn't get *his* treat until the gull gets *its*.

LEADER
(Still walking around in thoughtful circles) OK, OK. But what if the humans refuse to recognize us, and go on sacrificing to the gods first?

Y
Easy. You send sparrows to eat their corn. You send crows to drive their livestock crazy. Birds can be the most annoying creatures in the world when ... *(Seeing the look on LEADER'S face)* I mean ... nothing *personal* ... I mean ... you know, at *certain times* ...

LEADER
Allright, allright, — and if the humans *cooperate*?

X
You reward them. Send owls to eat the locusts who are eating the vine-blossoms. Send thrushes to devour the gnats who are attacking the figs ...

LEADER
They're already *doing* those things. No ... We must, I think, reward them *economically*. Yes, money is what they're really interested in ...

THE BIRDS
Gwendolyn MacEwen

HORNED GRUNCHEON
There's not very much... Mmmm, money in the realm of the birds, you know *(Staring at LEADER)* Is there. Come on now, — *is* there?

LEADER
(Quivering with rage) Well maybe not money, — meaning your stupid paper dollar, but ... *(Pausing)* ... a-Ha. Oh yes, — we have our eyes. We birds see what humans cannot see. We can see where the richest mines are located. We can point out all the best areas for speculators ... We, —

STAR-SPANGLED BANNER
(Stepping forward slowly) I thought that out years ago. It is a *very* lucrative endeavor. The human beings to the south of us were just *wild* when I sold them my sketches of the lands north of the *Metropolis*.

(The LEADER proceeds in the direction of THE STAR-SPANGLED BANNER, with murder in his eyes. The latter backs away, until he is trapped over The Sheer Drop, whence he takes wing, flapping furiously and screaming)

LEADER
(Returning to center stage) We birds have fore-knowledge of the weather, — isn't that so, Weathervane? (WEATHERANE *spins around happily a few times*)

LEADER
Meaning, of course,— we can aid and assist humans when it comes to forecasting storms, and so forth. This will cut down considerably on shipwrecks, and the humans will be highly indebted to us. Not to

THE BIRDS
Gwendolyn MacEwen

mention *buried treasure.* (Leering at X and Y, who are suddenly mesmerized) That's right, *mes amis,* — buried treasure. Oh yes, we birds know all the secret places. There are certain things that one can only see when one is very, very far removed. *Very* far removed either horizontally, or vertically. This is a distinct advantage, *n'est-ce pas?*

X
(*In a loud whisper to Y*) Let's forget about the Utopia thing. Let's go for the *buried treasure* ...

Y
Shut up! Can't you see that things are coming to a *head*?

LEADER
(*Stopping in his tracks and letting out a huge sigh of satisfaction*) Ah, I see it all before me. I see it all so clearly. It is ... *Utopia.*

Y
(*Whispering to X*) You see, you see? This is it. He's coming around to our way of seeing. We've got it, friend. We've found the answer. Freedom, here. (*X embraces Y and they dance around in ecstacy*)

LEADER
To think that I originally hated your guts, — you wonderful men. You've brought me the supreme revelation. A state, a state of being, an independent reality, a *realm* suspended in the regions between heaven

THE BIRDS
Gwendolyn MacEwen

and earth. I say to the gods, — Phooey. And to men, — Phooey. We are the birds. *Vive les oiseaux.*

RECITING BIRD
Les oiseaux.

TWO-IN-THE-BUSH
The birds, the birds.

EPOPS
(Confused, nervously making his way back into the Bush) Fine, yet ... Mmmm, let's get to it, shall we? Let's go inside and *discuss things*. Let's have a *meeting*, or a cabinet shuffle, or something, eh? *(He disappears in the Bush)* Is anyone coming in here with me? *(His voice recedes)* Eh? Is anyone interested in discussing things? ...

LEADER
Good, he's gone. Now we can get down to business.

X
Is that *fair*? I mean, he seemed like an allright sort, really ...

LEADER
A hopeless reactionary. Just hopeless. I knew the day would come when we would come to a parting of the ways ... Oh well, enough of that. Now, — down to business. First, we must think up a name for the new city, — something lofty and impressive ... What about *Smith's Falls!*

THE BIRDS
Gwendolyn MacEwen

X
Wuthering Heights

Y
The Plains of Abraham?

LEADER
Oh come on. Something suggesting light, and air and freedom. Something ecstatic, something *high*.

X
Grass City ...?

Y
No, that just silly. Wait ... I think I've got it. Yeh, yeh. Airy, and free, and high. Cloudsville, man, Cloudsville. (All of the birds cheer and clap wildly)

LEADER
I like it. I love it. It's Cloudsville, it's Cloudsville... *(Humming the words)* ... it almost sounds like a song. *(Turning to the birds)* Allright everybody, — hear this. We are now in the throes of establishing an absolutely *independent state,*— the realm of the birds. History is, even now, recording our every move. Think on that ... Now, first — *the wall. (To Y)* I appoint you my Minster of Wall Building, Town Planning, etc. etc., and whatever they call such things. Go and get the worker birds organized. We need mortar-mixers, sentinels ... you figure it out. Send messengers to the gods in heaven and to humans on earth. Tell them exactly what we are doing, and why. When you've finished,

THE BIRDS
Gwendolyn MacEwen

come back here. Take Metal Bird. He will show you where to go ...

Y
It's a huge job. Can't my friend come with me?

LEADER
We have other things to do here. *(Y exits with METAL BIRD pointing to some place offstage)* And now, and *now*, my friends, my countrymen, my countrybirds, my brothers and sisters ... *(Pacing back and forth in front of the birds dramatically)* ... now is the hour of our destiny. Now we enter a new age, the age of the *birds*, the age *(Pausing for effect)* ...of Aquarius. *(X frantically whispers something into his ear (LEADER coughing self-consciously)* Of course, I never said that Aquarius was a bird. Ha-ha. Certainly not. As we all know ... Aquarius was a fish. *(Some of the birds rush forward crying 'Fish, fish'. X gently eases them back)* I will begin again. This is the hour of our destiny. This is our *finest hour* ...

RECITING BIRD
(Stepping forward with an open book and pointing to some passage) That's been said before. It says right here that ... *(X pushes him back into the ranks of the other birds)*

LEADER
(Ignoring the last interruption) What I want to say is simply,— *this*. History is watching us. History is recording our every move. In any event, *somebody* is recording our every move ... Cloudsville. Cloudsville

THE BIRDS
Gwendolyn MacEwen

will be a model of the virtues afforded by only the highest of civilizations. Cloudsville will be Utopia, —, *Utopia*. *(He struts around the stage in ecstacy)* IN Cloudsville there will be a common goal. Peace. *(The birds cheer)* In Cloudsville there will be Happiness. *(The birds cheer)* In Cloudsville there will be Unity of Thought, and Unity of Action. There will be a 'One for All and All for One' over-riding feeling. *(The birds cheer)* There will be no 'provincial' or 'territorial' considerations. All that is past. *(He stops, due to the sudden cold silence on the part of the birds)*

X

What's wrong?

PURPLE-TAILED TERROR
(Shouting) He should know better. You don't talk to *birds* about abolishing *territorial* considerations.

X

I don't understand. I always thought that birds were free. You know, — even the old expression says it, —*free as birds*.

PURPLE-TAILED TERROR
That's rubbish. We would never have survived without what *he* calls 'territorial considerations'. Have you every really *watched* the birds, human? If you had, you'd know that *freedom* means drawing necessary lines around one's own territory. You fly *within* the lines you've drawn around yourself. Your freedom is also in the *drawing of those very lines.*

THE BIRDS
Gwendolyn MacEwen

X
I don't follow.

PURPLE-TAILED TERROR
I know you don't, human. And that's a shame. It's a shame because I wish I could teach *you* to fly *(The Birds are babbling among themselves and quibbling over the LEADER'S words)*

THE HORNED GRUNCHEON
(Grappling with THE SCARLET PIMPERNEL) I, personally, will defend my *territory* to the last tooth and claw ... You lousy Red!

THE SCARLET PIMPERNEL
(Resisting violently) When I get through with you, Gruncheon, you will not have tooth or claw to defend *anything* with. You reactionary scum!

LEADER
(Distressed) Gentlemen, gentlemen, gentlebirds, feathered friends, brothers ... STOP. *(There is a stunned silence)*

LEADER
(Wringing his hands) I only wanted to say that in Cloudsville ... there will be, — not only no territorial considerations, *but*,— no racial prejudice, no jealousy, no deceit, no lies. How beautiful, don't you see? And now ... let's get organized...

X
(Loudly, but to himself) This is starting to sound like the civilization I left. I'm scared. it sounds like the *Metropolis* ...

THE BIRDS
Gwendolyn MacEwen

SCARLET PIMPERNEL
I say Hurrah to the new city. Hurrah to our glorious leader. Hurrah, Hurrah, Hurrah. *(Several of the birds join in, until most of them are wildly cheering, 'no prejudice, no jealousy, no deceit, no lies. All for one and one for all.')*

LEADER
(Ecstatically) And to think this is only the beginning.

THE SHAMELESS HUSSY
(Sidling up to X) What are you doing tonight, stranger?

KISSING QUILL
(Outraged) Leave him alone. He's *mine*. *(SHAMELESS HUSSY and KISSING QUILL start plucking out one another's feathers. They are eventually separated by two birds, who lead them to opposite sides of the stage)*

LEADER
(Oblivious to whatever is happening around him) ... yes, only the beginning. What can I say? *The sky's the limit?* How marvellously *meaningful* everything becomes at times like these ... at times of Truth. Oh, we are embarking on a glorious, glorious venture ... *(The HORNED GRUNCHEON and THE SCARLET PIMPERNEL come to grips, and must be separated and deposited at opposite sides of the stage)*

X
(Alarmed, trying to divert attention away from LEADER's passionate speech) Don't you think we should have

THE BIRDS
Gwendolyn MacEwen

some kind of ceremony to consecrate the founding of the city?

LEADER
(Slowly turning to X) Oh, but yes. A ceremony, a consecration. How will we do it?

X
(Reaching into the large basket which he and Y originally brought in) It just so happens that my friend and I travelled fully prepared for such an occasion. In the event, we said to each other, that we find 'Utopia', we must have all the necessary symbolic articles on hand, so we perform a little ceremony and give thanks to the gods ... *(LEADER glares at him on hearing the last word)*

X
Ha ha ... a little joke I meant, of course,— a ceremony in which we give thanks to the *birds*. Yes ... now, what have we here? *(He erects a small 'altar' with a fold-out table from the basket: on it he slowly lays out various objects which he fishes out of the basket, — including a set of moose antlers and some large maple leaves.)* And now, an appropriate song ... before we sacrifice these various things ...

WEATHERVANE
(Stepping forward and leading off the song/chant) Praise the weathervanes, lords of the weather ....

HORNED GRUNCHEON
There's not much to be sure of in this cruel life. But one thing's for certain,— there'll *always* be weather.

THE BIRDS
Gwendolyn MacEwen

LE CROISSANT AND LA CREPE
Praise whatever is stunning and beautiful. Whatever is tasty and good.

PLASTIC BIRD
Praise what is neat, and functional.

ALARM COCK
Praise Time, which is of the essence.

CUCKOO CLOCK
Praise time, praise time, praise time ...

SHAMELESS HUSSY
Praise me, for whatever reason ...

(Running after SHAMELESS HUSSY) I'll kill her, I'll kill her.

SCARLET PIMPERNEL
Praise the measly Robin, the Spruce Grouse, The Tit-Mouse, the Wild-Eyed Whirly-Bird, The Starling, the Moonling, the Earthling.

PURPLE-TAILED TERROR
Praise the quiet workers and the quiet thinkers who one seldom sees ... *(Four eyes sparkle and gleam in the Bush)*

TWO-IN-THE-BUSH
Praise those of us who dwell forever in the bush ...

THE BIRDS
Gwendolyn MacEwen

X
(Getting caught up in the chanting) Praise the hawks, the god of the storks. Praise the swan, the mother of quails ... Praise the Pimpernel and the Spotted Pumpernickle. Praise moose-bird, beaver-bird and maple-bird.

LEADER
(Starting to chant, then abruptly stopping) Praise *who*?

X
Moose-bird, beaver-bird and maple-bird. They're symbolic.

LEADER
What?

X
They're... *emblematic* ...

LEADER
(To PURPLE-TAILED TERROR) What's he talking about?

PURPLE-TAILED TERROR
I'm not sure. I think he means that they're important, but they're not *birds* ... *(At this point, the hilarious chorus line which we have seen earlier dances back and forth across the stage a few times, then exits)*

LEADER
What was that, what *was* that?

THE BIRDS
Gwendolyn MacEwen

X
Never mind. Now, — let's prepare for sacrifice. *(He makes a big heap of the antlers, and leaves and pours oil over them)* I've got no matches. Does anyone have a light? *(The POET enters, with a guitar)*

POET
Hello there. Wow,— what have we here?

LEADER
Who are *you*?

POET
(Strumming a few chords) Who am I? *(Dreamily)* Who am I? I'm a poet, my friend. A tongue of honey. A slave of the Muse. I'm flying, man, I'm flying. That's why I came here. For pure *sound*. Fresh *insights*. New streams of consciousness. Dark, winding highways in the air ...

LEADER
Why *exactly* did you come here?

POET
Because life is nothingness. A hole within a hole. I want to be a bird. I want wings, *wings*. I want to dig *rarified* space. Clouds. Snow. Mist. I gotta find an atmosphere conducive to my work...

X
How can you work in the middle of a bunch of clouds?

THE BIRDS
Gwendolyn MacEwen

POET
They're the only place I can explore the real meaning of nothing-ness, the complexities of doom. You see,— I want to achieve a dense obscurity that's crystal clear. I want to perfect the art of saying Absolutely Nothing. I've got to examine the *Dynamics of Hopelessness*. Now do you understand?

LEADER
Not quite ... I mean ...

POET
Listen to this. I wrote it yesterday. You can see that I'm reaching a definitive breakthrough in my *stance*. I'm re-affirming the concept of language as a non-linear thing. God, it's so exciting. *(LEADER, X, and the other birds stare at each other in dismay, as the POET gives forth)*

POET
(Reciting) 'black black black black black night night night night night' What do you think? Is it too direct, too sexy? Is the world *ready* for it yet?

THE RECITING BIRD
I think it's still to *linear*. *(Looking at the others)* Don't you agree?

X
He's right. It's very *linear*.

LEADER
I agree that it's decidedly too *linear*. Have you got anything that goes around in circles, sort of?

THE BIRDS
Gwendolyn MacEwen

POET
Sure. I wrote some lines about this new city of yours. I thought it might turn out to be an opera. Or maybe a Haiku. It goes like this: 'turning and turning in the widening gyre, the falcon cannot hear the falconer ...'

THE RECITING BIRD
That's been done. You're a thief.

POET
I am not. I'm going through a sort of, you know, transitional period. I'm trying, among other things, to get *beyond language*.

X
I thought you were reaching a definitive breakthrough in your stance.

POET
(Screaming) Well can't I do both at the same time?

LEADER
Wait a minute. I have a question. How did you know about this new city? There hasn't been time for the news to travel ...

POET
(Vaguely) Time is like the wing of an eagle. *El condor passa.* *(He strums a few chords mysteriously)*

X
(To LEADER) The news has already leaked out. We're going to be overrun with types like him before we've even completed the city.

THE BIRDS
Gwendolyn MacEwen

POET
(Holding out his hand) All I say I say in the name of the Muse. A few dollars to help me on my way? Anything you can give will be appreciated. Peace. Love. All I want is to find my own little cloud.

X
(Handing him some money) Good luck. And now, leave us please. We have work to do.

POET
Thank you. Here's another poem, —

SCARLET PIMPERNEL
Enough, enough. *(Flapping his wings wildly and chasing the POET off stage)*

POET
Wait. This is a concrete poem. 'South wind, north wind, south wind, north wind, south wind ...' And there's another one too that's even better: 'grey morning, morning morning morning morning morning ... '

X
(Hurling a boulder after him) Here's some *concrete*. Take it.

POET
(Offstage) You'll be sorry. *(His voice fading away)* 'I saw the best minds of my generation ...'

X
(After a long pause in which all settle down) OK, let's get on with things. Does anyone have a light?

THE BIRDS
Gwendolyn MacEwen

RECITING BIRD
(Stepping forward shyly with a sheaf of papers and reading dramatically) 'The bird is on the wing. The grass is turning blue, and nations mumble. Let's get the whole world off the ground.'

X AND LEADER
(In one voice) What???

RECITING BIRD
I too, have written poetry ... *(Several of the other birds drag RECITING BIRD back into their ranks)*

X
OK, I'm asking you again. Does anyone have a *light*? Let's get this show on the road: let's get these sacrifices into the air. All I need is a *light*. *(The SEER enters, carrying a large golden book and a lantern. His costume is covered with signs of the zodiac and various magical symbols)*

SEER
Light, what is light but the paltry opposite of dark? *(Going over to X and holding the lantern close to his face)* And you, my son, are in great darkness ... *(He shines the lantern over the altar)* What is this? Preparations for a sacrifice. Stop everything. Let not the antlers of the moose be sacrificed.

LEADER
Who the Hell are *you*?

SEER
Guess.

THE BIRDS
Gwendolyn MacEwen

LEADER
I don't have time for guessing. *(Raising his voice)* I demand to know who you are and what you are doing here.

SEER
How dare you shout at me? I am a holy man. I am a seer. I am the book of the future. I have a prophecy which pertains to your new city.

LEADER
Why didn't you come and tell me *before* I started planning the city?

SEER
You can't have it both ways. The stars were against it.

LEADER
Allright, I'm listening. What's the prophecy?

SEER
(Opening the book and reading aloud) 'When the wolves and white crows congregate in Corinth ...'

X
What's *Corinth* got to do with anything?

SEER
That's what it says,— how should I know? *(Continuing)* ' ... and when the swallows return to Capistrano, — you shall sacrifice a pair of moose antlers. Then, and not before. *Meanwhile*, you shall give unto the prophet who reveals to you these words, some good

THE BIRDS
Gwendolyn MacEwen

food and wine, a new coat, and a decent pair of shoes. Money is optional, but vastly appreciated ...'

X
(Grabbing the book from him) Where does it say that?

SEER
Look for yourself. It's all in the Book.

X
There are other things 'in the Book'. 'If an impostor bugs you, throw him out.'

SEER
Where does it say that? Let me see ...

X
Look at the *Book*. Find out for yourself. *(He throws the Book at the SEER, who hurriedly exits)*

LEADER
Now let's by all means, get on with things. *(The SURVEYOR enters, carrying various complicated instruments, including a tripod, a large bent ruler, a huge compass and an equally huge magnifying glass)*

X
Who the Hell are you?

SURVEYOR
(Setting up tripod, wandering around measuring things, etc.) I've come to help you draw up plans for your

THE BIRDS
Gwendolyn MacEwen

new city, *('Measuring' X's head with the bent ruler and the compass, then peering into his eyes with the magnifying glass).* I'm a surveyor, as you can see. And a town planner. A frightfully accurate one, I might add.

X
Get that *thing* out of me eye. What are all these hideous metal things for, anyway?

SURVEYOR
(Proudly) Instruments for measuring the air. Yes indeed. I once wrote a superb thesis proving that air, — that is, *air in general,* as it were, — is shaped exactly like your average furnace.

LEADER
(To SCARLET PIMPERNEL) Let's get him out of here fast. He's dangerous. He's insane. He's a town planner, and they should all be locked up. Mad fiends, all of them. Mad fiends ... next thing we know he'll be talking about geodesic domes in the air, or four-lane skyways ... God knows what.

SURVEYOR
Yes,— exactly like your average furnace. Actually, using this amazing ruler, — *(Holding up the bent ruler)* — I was able to prove beyond a shadow of a doubt that space is curved. *(Pausing for effect)* Do you follow me?

X
No.

THE BIRDS
Gwendolyn MacEwen

PURPLE-TAILED TERROR
Actually, we birds have always known that space is *curved*. That's why we generally fly in arcs of one sort or another, rather than strictly straight lines.

SURVEYOR
(To X) Who's he?

X
He's a very philosophical bird. Anyway, *I* don't follow you, and I don't have all that much time to try ...

SURVEYOR
A pity. Oh well, here's how I plan to *do* your city, — *(LEADER and SCARLET PIMPERNEL surge forward to attack SURVEYOR, but the latter sidesteps without seeming to notice them, sending them sprawling on the ground)* ... Using my bent ruler, I'll draw a line from top to bottom, and then inscribe a circle with my compass from one of its points. Then, with a *straight* ruler, I'll describe a square within the circle, the centre of which will represent the market place, into which all the straight lines will lead, converging to this centre sort of like a star, which, although orbicular, sends forth its rays from all sides in straight lines. It's eminently simple. A triumph of pure geometry.

LEADER
Kill him.

THE BIRDS
Gwendolyn MacEwen

SCARLET PIMPERNEL
(*Helping LEADER up off the ground*) Here's what you can do with your *bent ruler*, you humanoid. (*He throws the tripod at SURVEYOR*)

LEADER
Go and survey something else, you *outsider*. (*The SURVEYOR exits. SCARLET PIMPERNEL and LEADER throw the rest of his instruments, plus a couple of rocks, after him*)

RECITING BIRD
(*Stepping forward with the usual formality and quoting from his book*) 'Weak mortals, chained to the earth, creatures of clay as frail as the foliage of the woods, the illusion of a dream, harken to us, who are immortal beings, ethereal, ever young and occupied with thoughts of eternity, for ...' (*Other birds pull RECITING BIRD back into their ranks. Suddenly the sky darkens, and there is a great buzzing and humming*)

X
What is it? What's happening?

PURPLE-TAILED TERROR
Oh no, it's, — it's *them*.

Y
Who's *them*? (*The BIRDS twitter and become panicky. The buzzing and humming gets worse*)

THE BIRDS
Gwendolyn MacEwen

LEADER
It's *them*,— the most dreaded enemy of all. It's ... *the wasps*. (*Many birds scream with fear*)

SCARLET PIMPERNEL
The *wasps* are coming. (*The other birds become hysterical, running about and colliding into one another*)

BIRDS
The wasps are coming, the wasps are coming. (*The stage becomes totally black: the sound of bees is prevalent for a moment or two. Then, utter silence. Lights up*)

LEADER
(*Slowly*) Was anyone stung?

X
What was all that about, anyway?

LEADER
Nothing. The birds and the bees. (*Pausing, then laughing*) You don't understand. A ... minor dispute over *who* controls *which* highways of the air ...

X
(*Obviously shaken*) Are you trying to tell me that ... that ... you have traffic problems. *Traffic* problems? Up *here*? I mean, isn't it enough that the birds have bloody *territorial* disputes? What else? You have to cope with the wasps? Are you trying to tell me that all this is *real*?

THE BIRDS
Gwendolyn MacEwen

LEADER
(Sadly) Are you trying to believe any different, *mon ami?*

X
(Slowly and sadly) Are you suggesting that ... even Utopia is not *Utopia?*

LEADER
I'm suggesting nothing. My wise compatriot, Epops, half-human and half-bird, who only recently disappeared into the Bush, would probably have agreed with what I have to say ...

X
Which is ...?

LEADER
(Sighing) That even Utopia ... is not Utopia ... *(X and LEADER stare at one another mournfully. Then, something which looks like a large orange balloon comes slowly in)*

PEKING DUCK
Where is he, where's our leader?

LEADER
Ah, it's you, Peking Duck. What news?

PEKING DUCK
It's almost finished, it's almost finished. The great wall is almost finished.

THE BIRDS
Gwendolyn MacEwen

LEADER
(Warily) What do you mean ... *almost?*

PEKING DUCK
It's beautiful. It's magnificent. It's wider than any *highway* I've ever seen. It's simply enormous. It rivals the Great Wall of China, it, —

X
Wait a minute. That was pretty fast work, wasn't it? I mean from the time my friend left with Metal Bird to start organizing work on the wall ...

PEKING DUCK
You don't understand. Time flies, time just *flies* in Cloudsville. *(He starts dancing gaily around with various birds)*

LEADER
(Drawing him aside) There is something which you're not telling me, my friend. I demand to know, — why is the wall only *almost* finished?

PEKING DUCK
How should I know?

LEADER
(Grabbing him by the throat) I'll cook your goose, Peking Duck. I mean, — pardon me, — I'll strangle you if you don't tell me.

PEKING DUCK
OK, I'll tell. The wall is not finished because ... there's been a strike.

THE BIRDS
Gwendolyn MacEwen

X
(Screaming) A strike. Among the birds. Are you serious. I'll kill myself. We have not escaped the *Metropolis*. It's the same here, the same. Let me die, I want to die.

SHAMELESS HUSSY
(Putting a wing around his shoulders) Let's fly away, you and I. Away from all this

KISSING QUILL
(Tackling SHAMELESS HUSSY head on and knocking her to the ground) Back off, bitch. He's mine, I tell you. He's mine. *(SHAMELESS HUSSY and KISSING QUILL are separated and led to opposite sides of stage)*

LEADER
For God's sake, what happened? Why a *strike*, of all things? And why now? *Now*, when our destiny awaits us? Why, *why*?

HORNED GRUNCHEON
Imbécile! You do not see the truth even when it's pasted in front of your eyes? Money, *mon ami*, money.

PEKING DUCK
Money, yes. Other things too. Greed. Suspicion. Some birds were offered higher wages than others ...

X
On the basis of *what*?

PEKING DUCK
How should I know? Color, creed, whatever. Immigrant status...

THE BIRDS
Gwendolyn MacEwen

X
Immigrant status? What the Hell is that? What the Hell does that mean in the realm of the birds.

LEADER
(Patiently informing him) Some birds migrated and ended up here, as landed birds, do you see? They were then granted a thing called Immigrant status. So, as long as they refused to fly, — to fly their coop, so to speak — they were granted the privilege of living in our domain.

PEKING DUCK
All I know is that the *citizen birds* are demanding higher wages than the *landed birds*. You figure it out.

LEADER
This is preposterous. We must at all costs get on with the wall. Who are the dissenters?

PEKING DUCK
I have not prepared a list, but I can, if you like ...

LEADER
Whoever they are, *ground them*. If they try to escape, don't grant them permission to land, once they're airborne. Keep them in holding patterns, *forever*.

X
Aren't you being a bit ... strenuous? I mean, all this is giving me an awful *déjà vu*. This was the way things were when we left the *Metropolis* ...

THE BIRDS
Gwendolyn MacEwen

LEADER
(*On the defensive*) Don't be silly. We have no social problems here. We have no racial problems here. This is a free society. Everybody's *flying*.

X
I don't believe you, you know ...

PEKING DUCK
The wall's going to be ... O, millions of inches long. I measured it myself. The cranes did the groundwork. Thirty thousand of them came with stones for the foundations. Then, ten thousand storks came to make the bricks. The geese used their feet like spades to empty the mortar into the troughs. It was so exciting.

LEADER
So it seems there was no lack of teamwork ...

PEKING DUCK
There was no lack of teamwork. Just riots. I mean, great *discord*. (*Pausing*) Then, things got somewhat out of control. The swallows returned to Capistrano, and, —

LEADER
What? That's *important*.

PEKING DUCK
Yes, and then ... well, some of the birds flew their coop, but,—

THE BIRDS
Gwendolyn MacEwen

X
Yes, yes , go on.

PEKING DUCK
Well you see, everything was happening at *once*. The pelicans were using their beaks to square off the gates. Others were securely bolting the bolts. Your human friend was posting sentinels just about *everywhere*, and ordering beacons to be lit on the ramparts ...

LEADER
And then, and *then* ...?

PEKING DUCK
Well, there was some of sort of *leak* in the *gates* ... I mean ... I mean ...

X
Do you mean,—?

PEKING DUCK
Yes. Precisely. An *air-gate*.

X
Just what we bloody need. An air-gate. *(LEADER throws himself on the ground, plucks out his feathers, and weeps)*

PEKING DUCK
Then everything became, became, well, pandemonium. I don't remember what happened first. But sud-

THE BIRDS
Gwendolyn MacEwen

denly, all the birds were shrieking at each other in separate dialects ...

X

That does it. Bloody tower of Babel all over again.

LEADER

I *knew* we should have discussed language rights before we went blindly ahead with the Wall. I knew it, *mon Dieu*, I just knew it.

PEKING DUCK

Yes, well, — after that, or maybe it was *before* ... some bird, I've forgotten which, screamed something like: 'What's this Cloudsville all about anyway? Who ever asked us if we wanted an independent state or not? There wasn't even a referendum.'

X

Then what ...?

PEKING DUCK

Then all Hell broke loose. And to make matters worse, some *gods* noticed the confusion and seized the opportunity to slip through the air-gate. They got past the jays who were supposedly on guard ...

LEADER

(Groaning) Which gods?

THE BIRDS
Gwendolyn MacEwen

PEKING DUCK
I don't know. The gods all look alike to me. These ones were winged, though. I think. Anyway, some of the birds who were supposed to be patrolling the Wall tried to go after them, but in the general chaos they ended up colliding into one another. It was all just *insane*. (*Offstage there is a buzzing sound which swiftly intensified: in the final stage it resembles the whining scream of jet engines after an aircraft touches down*)

SHAMELESS HUSSY
I think it's an invasion from Outer Space! Oh, how thrilling. (*Hopeless commotion as the birds attempt to gather their forces behind X and LEADER*)

LEADER
Fall in, fall in. We're being attacked. Don't panic. Reason things out first, then panic. Remember, this might mean war. We must defend the air. Keep your eyes peeled, whatever that means.

HORNED GRUNCHEON
(*Reeling to stage front and collapsing*) I can't stand violence. I can't bear the sight of blood ...

X
They're *coming*. Assume defense position. (*The birds extend their wings*)

X
Ready, set ... go. (*The birds fold their wings over themselves and their immediate neighbors. The final effect is

THE BIRDS
Gwendolyn MacEwen

that of a multi-colored dome) A GODDESS enters with plastic wings studded with sequins. She carries an AIR CANADA flight bag. She is on roller skates, and her entrance is so swift that she can't stop, but goes zooming across the stage and over the Sheer Drop. She immediately re-enters and stops in mid-stage)

GODDESS

(Talking to herself) This can't be the right place ...

X
(Timidly emerging from the 'dome' and approaching her) Who are you? How did you get here?

GODDESS
The gods move in mysterious ways ...

LEADER
(Also emerging from the 'dome') I don't care how they move. They're not permitted to come here without a passport. This is an independent and unknown state. Let's not mess around, eh?

X
You could be killed for trespassing, you know ...

GODDESS
It wouldn't work, I'm immortal.

LEADER
You could be torn apart, piece by piece ...

THE BIRDS
Gwendolyn MacEwen

GODDESS
That wouldn't work either. We gods and goddesses are like plants and octopii and starfish, and such. We grow new parts. When necessary.

X
OK, OK. Why are you here?

GODDESS
I've a message to deliver. A message from Zeus. He finds the idea of your 'independent state' abhorrent and intolerable.

LEADER
Mon Dieu.

X
(Cursing and waving his arms wildly) Holy God. *(There is some commotion offstage. Y and METAL BIRD enter. They are weary and bedraggled)*

Y
(Embracing X) It's OK, friend,— we're back ...

LEADER
(To GODDESS) Men now worship the birds as gods, and it is to *them*,—by God — that they will offer their sacrifices. From now on, *everything is for the birds.* *(Pausing in dismay)*

GODDESS
You're cuckoo. Lightning will strike you dead. Zeus will strike you down for your insolence. It is written.

THE BIRDS
Gwendolyn MacEwen

LEADER
Who ever said that the gods could read or write?

GODDESS
(Momentarily losing her balance on her skates, and flailing her arms in the air) Blasphemy. You'll pay for this. *(Y gives her a slap on the ass, which sends her zooming out)*

LEADER
Well done, well done. We will not tolerate insolence in Cloudsville. Let the gods know that we mean *business*.

Y
(Casually) What gods, man? They all look alike to me ...

PEKING DUCK
Me too. That's what I just said ...

LEADER
O shut up! What's that got to do with anything? *(To Y)* Now,—tell me ... what news? What news since *he* *(Pointing to PEKING DUCK) got here?*

Y
(Shrugging) We left things the same way he did. I mean, you know, — the screaming and shrieking, the rioting. Everybody talking about color all of a sudden. Everybody going weird all at once. Just like back home in the Metropolis ... *(Nudging X)* ... isn't that so, my friend? Isn't it just like back home, eh,— eh? *(He bursts out laughing. Uncontrollably)* It's like

THE BIRDS
Gwendolyn MacEwen

we haven't even left. It's wild. We haven't escaped anything, brother.

METAL BIRD
(Stepping forward) That's the bad news. But he didn't say anything about the good news.

LEADER
I'm all ears.

METAL BIRD
The good news is what we heard on the way back here. People in the *Metropolis* have heard about Cloudsville, and the idea has simply blown their minds. *Everybody* wants to come and live here. I tell you, it's *insane*. I heard that they're all starting to wear artificial wings. It's hysterical. They're starting to give themselves bird-names, and they're singing bird-songs. The *Metropolis* has gone mad. That's what I heard ...

X
Don't tell me the rest. I can guess. A bunch of them are probably on their way here right now, right?

METAL BIRD
Right. What luck, eh? Prosperity comes to Cloudsville. Money. Tourist dollars. *(All of the birds begin to flap their wings and converse. We catch parts of their conversations)*

PLASTIC BIRD
Well, nothing as extreme as a gambling casino, *but,* —

THE BIRDS
Gwendolyn MacEwen

LE CREPE
... A couple of nice little cafés, perhaps ...

CUCKOO CLOCK
A few really precious little antique stores ...

SHAMELESS HUSSY
At least one decent strip joint ... *(X joins Y who is still weeping. Arms over one another's shoulders, they slowly walk back and forth across the stage, sobbing)*

LEADER
What's going on? What the Hell's going on?

PURPLE-TAILED TERROR
Madness is going on. As always. Men are fools. Birds are fools. The gods are fools.

SCARLET PIMPERNEL
That doesn't satisfy me. I'm leaving. Don't anybody try to stop me. *(He looks around and realizes nobody is listening)* OK, everybody ... I'm *leaving*. Don't anybody try to *stop me*. *(He flies out over the Sheer Drop and X and Y stop in their tracks)*

X
Someone's coming... *(PROMETHEUS enters, wearing dark sunglasses and a travel bag labelled Cosmic Tours, Inc.)*

PROMETHEUS
(Approaching X and Y) I can hardly see a thing through these glasses. I wonder ... can you, er, — take

THE BIRDS
Gwendolyn MacEwen

me to your Leader? (Pausing) I know that's been done before. It happens to be true. I truly want to see your Leader.

Y
Who are you? You don't look like a bird, a human, or a god...

PROMETHEUS
That's because I'm travelling *incognito*. See? *(Pointing to his bag)* Cosmic Tours, *Inc. Incognito.*

X
Who are you?

PROMETHEUS
(Pausing dramatically) I'm a human who defied the gods. I ended up with an eagle picking at my liver ...

X AND Y AND LEADER
(Simultaneously) Prometheus. *(Prometheus opens up a transparent umbrella and holds it over himself, X and Y. Leader also sneaks under)*

PROMETHEUS
Ssshh. Don't say my name out loud. OK, now we are safe. Listen. I am here to tell you that Zeus is in serious trouble. According to the latest news from the *Metropolis*, the people now want to worship and make sacrifices to, — yes, — the *birds*, not the gods. You can guess what that means. Yes. The gods will *starve*.

THE BIRDS
Gwendolyn MacEwen

LEADER
(Chuckling) A pity.

PROMETHEUS
Allright. My advice to you is this. When they, the gods, send their emissaries down here to bargain with you ... bear in mind, — they are half-starved. Seize your advantage. They are *ravenous* ... do you understand?

LEADER
Quite.

X
OK, but, —

Y
Right on, *but* ... what happens when we make peace with the *gods*, man? And after how do we make peace with *man*, man?

X
Exactly. What do we do with all the people from the *Metropolis*? All the eager tourists? All the humans who long to be birds? Eh? *(A long silence)*

PURPLE-TAILED TERROR
(Wearily) Easy. Bring them down to earth. Disillusion them, as man and bird and beast has been disillusioned since time began. Clip their wings. Ground them.

THE BIRDS
Gwendolyn MacEwen

PROMETHEUS
(Exiting) I go. Goodbye. Good luck.

X
(To PURPLE-TAILED TERROR) You know what you just said, don't you? You said, in effect, to undo everything we've begun. To return to normal,— whatever that is. To be, in fact, our usual bungling, imperfect selves ...

PURPLE-TAILED TERROR
Sad, isn't it? But that is what I meant. Maybe it's just too soon for any of us to try to surpass our shortcomings. Birds, men, whoever ...

Y
(Bleakly) So there are no idyllic kingdoms, there are no Utopias, there are no perfect places ... *(Pauses, and then screams)* Well can't there even be something that's just plain nice. OK, maybe we set our goals too high, maybe we dreamed impossible dreams, maybe we built castles in the air ... But is it too much to ask of life that it become just a *little bit better*, for God's sake. Just a little bit nice? Is that asking too much, gods, is it? *(He kneels and implores heaven for an answer)*

SHAMELESS HUSSY
I'm nice, honey. Don't you think *I'm* nice...?

Y
Go away, whore of Babylon. Besides, I only go for *women*.

THE BIRDS
Gwendolyn MacEwen

SHAMELESS HUSSY
(Bursts into hysterical tears)

LEADER
(To Y) Look, that was just a bit *much*, don't you think? Male chauvinistic off-colored human pig. Bird-hater.

X
(To LEADER) You can't talk to my friend like that. *(The Birds start fighting among themselves, splitting up into groups which are either pro or con X and Y)*

RECITING BIRD
(Stepping to stage front, oblivious of the commotion) O thrice happy race of airy birds. Mere words cannot express our happiness. Our leader is brighter than the brightest star that illumines the earth. Perfumes of unspeakable sweetness pervade the ethereal realms, and clouds of incense waft in light whirlwinds before the breath of the zephyr...

LEADER
I wish that once, just once, you'd say something that made sense ... That has nothing to do with *anything*.

A BIRD
Make him stop, make him stop. *(THE RECITING BIRD is dragged to the ground, and he continues to spout forth poetic nonsense from his prone position. Suddenly, there is a roar of thunder. Total silence. Then a flash of lightning and another thunder clap. The god POSEIDON enters, resplendent with jewels. He carries an airline flight*

THE BIRDS
Gwendolyn MacEwen

bag with OLYMPIC AIRWAYS *in large white letters inscribed upon it. He is followed by* HERACLES, *who trails the remnants of a parachute behind him and who wears a T-shirt inscribed with* MT. OLYMPUS DARE-DEVILS)

POSEIDON
So this is the headquarters for 'Cloudsville' *(To HERACLES, loudly, so that all can hear)* What's our plan of action, Heracles.

HERACLES
(Flexing his muscles) Well, Poseidon, first, I strangle the guy who thought about building the wall. *(X, Y, and LEADER are slowly shrinking toward The Sheer Drop; the other birds are joining them, inching away from POSEIDON and HERACLES)*

POSEIDON
Let's not be cruel. I've heard that, among other things, Cloudsville is supposed to be a place of *peace*. And let's not forget that we were sent here as ambassadors of peace ... *(There is a buzzing and whispering sound from within the circle of birds. Gradually, the birds disband and take up new positions around the stage, leaving X, Y and LEADER alone, close to the Sheer Drop. To our amazement, they are cooking something in a cauldron over a fire)*

LEADER
(Stirring the contents of the cauldron with a large wooden spoon, and pretending, —along with the other,— to be

THE BIRDS
Gwendolyn MacEwen

unaware of the presence of POSEIDON and HERACLES) I have always believed, *mes amis*, that the way to a man's heart, — or for that matter, an enemy's heart, or even a god's heart,— is in fact through his stomach. *Eh bien* ... Perhaps that is a foolish idea. It is a foolish idea,—*ne c'est pas?*

X
(Also stirring) I can't say for sure. But I do know that when all else fails, a little feast never hurts. *(Consulting his COOKBOOK)* Let's see now ... I'll need a cheese-grater ... *(Reading aloud from book)* ... 'Sautée onions and celery over medium heat until golden brown. Ease in your thinly-sliced baby mushrooms, one by one ...'

LEADER
(Jumping up and down with delight) Magnifique! The *champignons* will be superb.

Y
(Also stirring) I'm beginning to understand your *logic*, my friends. We will dine first,— like the great kings and conquerors of old. We will dine, and *then* dream our dreams, and *then* carve out our empires, and *then* construct with so much Love, and so much Hope, our possible Utopias...

POSEIDON
(In a commanding voice) We have come to see you. We have come from the home of the gods.

THE BIRDS
Gwendolyn MacEwen

LEADER
(Ignoring him) In just a minute we have the *perfect* sauce ...

HERACLES
(Peering into the cauldron, faint from hunger) What's .. what's *cooking* ...?

X
(Feigning surprise) Oh, nothing really. A sort of variation on a fairly complicated Tetrazzini. An unusual recipe. *(Reading from cookbook)* Dash of cayenne. Parsley sprig ... that should come later ... Hmmm. ...

POSEIDON
(Assuming an aggressive stance) I, Poseidon, have come with Heracles, from Mount Olympus to tell you , in the name of Zeus, that *the gods do not want war.*

Y
(Ignoring his words) Damn, we're out of cooking oil ...

HERACLES
Who cares? I'm starving ... let's eat.

POSEIDON
(Stiffening) I've been instructed to tell you that ... *(Hesitating in embarrassment)* that the feud is over, that is, the feud between the birds and the gods,— due to the fact that the gods are starving.

THE BIRDS
Gwendolyn MacEwen

HERACLES
That's it, then. Let's eat.

POSEIDON
You're not even a real *god*,— you, half human. I'm more starving than you. *(HERACLES and POSEIDON make a dive for the cauldron. X and Y hold them back)*

LEADER
(Still stirring with his wooden spoon) If you'll all just act like civilized beings ... I might invite you all to dinner. *(There is a pause, while everybody, including the Birds, chatters and 'preens")*

PURPLE-TAILED TERROR
Let's be frank. We're all very hungry.

KISSING QUILL
I don't have a *thing* to wear ...

SHAMELESS HUSSY
(Throwing herself upon WEATHERVANE) Marriages were made in heaven ...

HERACLES
Full power to the birds. Let's eat.

LEADER
(To X) What else does the recipe call for?

THE BIRDS
Gwendolyn MacEwen

X
Hmm ... clarified butter .. and ... *(He pauses)* ... a generous dose of *peace*...

Y
Peace, brothers ... peace at all costs. *(A long thoughtful silence)*

HERACLES
I was instructed to ask you a very important question ...

LEADER
What question, my muscular friend?

HERACLES
(Pausing) What's for dessert?

X
Honey-cakes, you fool. Your favorite. *(The Birds spontaneously break into a dance)*

LEADER
So ... The gods are placated. The humans have had their fun. And everything returns to what we must call 'normal'.

Y
Not really. *(To PURPLE-TAILED TERROR)* What would *you* say, my philosophical friend? Is there such a thing as a 'best of all possible worlds?'

THE BIRDS
Gwendolyn MacEwen

PURPLE-TAILED TERROR
There is, in my understanding, a *present* world, a world we live in here and now. It offers all the questions, and provides some of the answers ...

CUCKOO CLOCK
(Timidly stepping forward) Isn't it maybe a question of *occupying* the present, sort of moment by moment, tick by tick ...?

WEATHERVANE
Or something like, well as simple as, — just knowing where you *stand*, and which direction you're pointing towards?

X
(Caught up in the dancing) Who cares, who cares? In a very strange way, we've flown around in circles, and finally come back home.

Y
(Also dancing) Maybe you're right, friend. Isn't the world just like a kaleidoscope ... a bunch of colors and miracles going round and round ...

LEADER
OK. I invite you *all* to dine.

RECITING BIRD
(Stepping forward as usual) O dance, dance. Grace and beauty. The birds are called to glorious destinies. O

THE BIRDS
Gwendolyn MacEwen

celebrate the thunder that shakes the earth, the flaming lightning of Zeus and his flashing thunderbolts ... *(The BIRDS drag him back, loudly protesting, into the dance. Lightning and thunder follow)*

RECITING BIRD
(Gasping for breath) O ye divine shafts of flame. O ye rolling thunder. Praise the gods. Praise the birds. Praise everyone. *(The BIRDS fall together in a heap, twittering and laughing feathers flying everywhere)*

THE BIRDS
Gwendolyn MacEwen

PRINTED IN CANADA